AFFIRMATIONS OF A PRICELESS JEWEL

PRICELESS JEWELS™

© 2018 Priceless Jewels
All rights reserved.

ISBN 978-0-692-12404-8

No part of this publication may be reproduced, stored in a retrieval system, or transmitted in any form or by any means, electronic, mechanical, photocopying, recording, or otherwise, without written permission of the publisher. For information regarding permission, write to [insert publisher information].

## FORWARD

Affirmations of a Priceless Jewel is a beautiful journey of discovering the many facets of your true value. God is radically pursuing you with His unconditional love and NOW is the time to receive every good thing that He has for you.

**THESE PAGES ARE FULL OF INSPIRATIONAL TRUTHS TO HELP YOU RISE ABOVE EVERYTHING THAT PREVIOUSLY LABELED OR DEFINED YOU.**

Kristine Jones invites you into her story and shares wisdom from very real experiences so that you can find a greater measure of confidence & boldness. Her words will fire you up to shake off fears, insecurities, shame and anything from your past that has hindered you or made you feel stuck. You will be repositioned to the place of royalty that you were originally fashioned for.

Through reading this book, you will quickly find that you love yourself more and that nothing is impossible for you when you believe. You are loved, beautiful, powerful, eternally accepted and priceless!

*Sula Skiles*
Pastor, Author, and Sex Trafficking Abolitionist

## PREFACE

My two girls and my son are the motivations behind this book as well as my wishing that I had a woman like me growing up. I remember growing up and having no identity and no clue as to who I was or where I was going. I searched for acceptance anywhere I could get it. Affirmations of A Priceless Jewel is a book that will prompt you to search yourself, forgive yourself, and flush out all of the negativity that was once there. I believe this is a book that will give you daily affirmations about how priceless you are and help you to understand that you were created by God with love and for a purpose.

I would first like to thank God for pouring His love on me. No matter where I am in my life, He is always there. I want to thank my husband, Michael Jones, for loving me when I am wrong and when I am right. Mike, you are always that constant example of God's expression of His love; you've continued to show me how precious I am. To my sister Darlene and my brother Thomas, thank you for always supporting me and having my back even when I messed up majorly. You both have been there for me through so much and I am so thankful. To my dad, thank you for showing me how to be real, authentic, to never give up, for helping me at any moment, for supporting me, and teaching me how to be independent and strong. To my mom in heaven, you are the greatest example of a strong woman, loving mom, and a true fighter. I miss you so much and am grateful for the time I did get to have with you. To my girls and my son, thank you for your daily love and helping me to deny myself. You make my day and are God's divine blessings in my life. You make me better every second of the day. To Mrs. Debbie, my spiritual mom, who guided me growing up when I had no mother, you as a strong black woman, were what I aspired to be; at youth ministry, you showed me who Jesus really is and that is LOVE. Thank you for always being there for me and my sister and being such a beautiful woman of God. As a spiritual mother, you kept us on the right path even when we fell off. To my friend Janelle, thank you and your hubby for supporting the vision God gave me for the Priceless Jewels group. Thanks for pushing me to start the group and to share what was in me with other women. To all the ladies of Priceless Jewels, thank you for allowing me to be me and allowing me to grow with you as we stepped outside of our boxes. To my Pastors Creflo and Taffi Dollar, thank you for teaching the Word of God with such simplicity that I got it! Thank you for allowing me to serve you in ministry and with Radical Women's Ministry. This ministry helped to change my life and I am so grateful for the prayers that sent me to the Chapel on Easter Sunday when you taught from Genesis to Revelations about the birth, death, and resurrection of Jesus;
why it took place the way it did; and how much He loved us.
This changed my life!!Thank you for being you!

contents

| | |
|---|---|
| Why Are You Beautiful | 4 |
| God Loves You This Much | 14 |
| Never Give Up | 24 |
| Confidence | 36 |
| The Priceless Jewel | 46 |
| Beauty From The Inside Out | 52 |
| The Greatest Fashion | 64 |
| Be Bold | 70 |
| You Are Forgiven | 76 |
| Who Am I | 84 |
| Prayer | 92 |

# Priceless
## price·less (adjective)

*¹So precious that its value cannot be determined*

# Jewel
## jew·el (noun)

*¹a precious stone, typically a single crystal or a piece of a hard lustrous or translucent mineral, cut into shape with flat facets or smoothed and polished for use as an ornament.*

*²one that is highly esteemed*

When I think of a Priceless Jewel, I think of a young woman whom God is reshaping, smoothing out, and refining herself to show the world His beautiful ornament. She is rare, uncommon, unique, and custom made!

This book is a reminder of just how special you are and that you are God's Priceless Jewel.

A capable, intelligent, and virtuous woman- who is he who can find her? She is far more precious than jewels and her value is far above rubies or pearls.

Priceless. (n.d.) In Oxford Living Dictionaries. Retrieved from https://en.oxforddictionaries.com/definition/priceless

Jewel. (n.d.) In Google. Retrieved from https://www.google.com/#q=jewel+definition

Jewel. (n.d.) In Merriam-Webster dictionary. Retrieved from https://www.merriam-webster.com/dictionary/jewel

01
CHAPTER ONE

# Why you are beautiful?
## You are custom made.

Oh yes, you shaped me first inside, then out; you formed me in my mother's womb. I thank you, High God—you're breathtaking! Body and soul, I am marvelously made! I worship in adoration—what a creation! You know me inside and out, you know every bone in my body; You know exactly how I was made, bit by bit, how I was sculpted from nothing into something. Like an open book, you watched me grow from conception to birth; all the stages of my life were spread out before you, The days of my life all prepared before I'd even lived one day.

Psalm 139:13-16 (MSG)

When I started looking at the word beautiful, I loved how a girlfriend of mine, Jamila, said, "Be U to the Full!" I started to think about this. Be U—who you are and all of who you are to the fullest. Whereas the dictionary definition of beautiful is "pleasing to the senses or mind, a very high standard, excellent," I like my friend's definition better. See, the world has always tried to hold us to its standard of beauty, with its photoshopped images on magazine covers and billboards. This makes young women, girls, and even more mature woman feel like they have to be shaped a certain way and even be a certain weight. This is what I struggled with for years—my identity—wondering if I was pretty and attractive enough. Wondering if I was good enough? Fine enough? Or if I met the standard of a beautiful woman. I was in constant pursuit of being what "they" said was beautiful, even to the point of trying to mimic what I saw.

As I glanced back over my life, I would say it all started when I was around 9-years-old. My mom got me started in modeling. I was always in the mirror dancing, posing, or trying on clothes. Once I started at the modeling school, my teacher noticed how confident I was walking the runway. I began to help the kids learn how to confidently walk on the runway. I was always someone else when I was up there. In my mind, I was a super star. The funny thing is I was not very confident inside at all. As I got older and continued in the modeling industry, I was not ready for what was coming in this superficial world of fashion, especially always hearing how pretty you have to be and how looks are everything. This made me think the only thing that mattered was beauty.

But to a 9-year-old or 12-year-old, what is beauty? See people often told me how pretty I was, how my hair was so long and beautiful, how my skin was like creamy milk, but I never saw it that way. Being a multi-racial child from a German mother and African-American and Cherokee Indian father, I felt like I never fit in. I never felt pretty enough. At my fashion shows and photoshoots, I would hear compliment after compliment on how pretty, how gifted I was, how unique my walk was, or how the camera loved me. Inside, I was empty and void of loving myself. I craved taking pictures and modeling because I was always complimented. I felt pretty all made up. The only time I felt like I was somebody was when the attention was on me. This was a lonely place—to feel the need to have constant attention from whatever source was willing to give it.

As I grew up, the modeling world became more superficial. I could become anyone I wanted to on that runway. Someone prettier, thicker, taller, but never myself. This led to how I saw myself in friendships and relationships, especially when I started dating in high school.

I remember hearing, "You cute but not bad enough". My peers picked on me and called me "ruler," "paper," or "pencil" and oh the infamous "Olive Oyl." Now ya'll know even though Brutus and Popeye fought over her. To make things worse, I wore a bun a lot lol!!! When I would watch the show, I would search for something pretty in her, but each time I just saw the same ol' dress and bun. Was I Olive Oyl or was I unique? To top off the name calling, guess what? Yep, I had really bad acne and was called "pizza face" and other names. This did not help me out one bit in the area of self-confidence or beauty. Nor did the fact that I was multi-racial growing up in the South. As a model, I had a few jobs here and there; hair shows were always easy because I had lots of long pretty hair. But when it came to booking an ad, I just wasn't enough for any agency I went to. As I got older, I realized that I just wasn't what they were looking for. This greatly damaged my perception of beauty. Often, I acted or carried myself as if I was all that but deep down inside, I always had these lingering questions and damaging thoughts about myself.

## Am I enough? Am I pretty? What is wrong with me?

*Maybe if I was all German or all African American, I would be attractive. Maybe if I was thicker I would be desirable?*

At some point, you begin to do things to get attention or to feel beautiful by seeking out compliments from boys or wearing things to hear someone say a nice word or two. The reality is that even though they would say it often, they didn't mean it and the bottom line is if I don't believe it, nothing anyone can say will make me feel better. You can call people pretty all day, compliment their hair, shoes, makeup, and anything else about them but if they don't think so, it will go in one ear and out the other while they question what makes them beautiful? Sometimes, a person may even ask: If I am so beautiful, a nice dresser and smart then why am I alone, or why did this person leave me or why don't people treat me better? Why did he cheat on me if I am all that? Why didn't the agency sign me if I am so pretty?

All the *whys* come in when you don't know who you are deep down within and when you haven't accepted who you are created to be and how God created you. What we have to realize is when God creates, He doesn't make mistakes or dysfunctional things. Everything He makes is customized and intricately detailed. Look at the ocean, the palm tree, the lotus flower that grows in the murkiness of the swamps or rivers. It is covered in mud and water, but once it grows up out of the murk, you behold such a beautiful flower. Look at the colors of the sunset—a canvas of His expression of colors. Look at how the butterfly is formed; it starts out as a caterpillar, then creates a cocoon, and when it's due season comes, the butterfly flourishes into a beautiful creature with markings that define its name. These are small examples of the beauty God creates, just like He took His time to create you.

From your hair to your toes, each part of you is customized and shaped by His hands. Isn't that so amazing that God handpicked you before this world was formed (Ephesians 1:4-5)?

*God loves you just the way you are;*

## *you are precious to Him and set apart from all the rest.*

There is no one else in this entire universe that looks like you, talks like you, walks like you, or sounds like you. Look at yourself in the mirror; see how each detail of you is beautiful. OK, you're probably like Kristine, I don't see it! Well GET UP! Go to your closest mirror; go now! I'm so serious, get up, and go do this with me. If you're on lunch break reading this or on a train, pull out a mirror. If you don't have one, use your phone's camera. Yes, do it now.

OK, so now we are here looking at the mirror, look past your eyes, your lashes, and your makeup (if you're wearing any). What do you see? Say this with me: I am beautiful. Tell yourself again that you are beautiful. Now, tell yourself why. I know this may be hard or you may say *Kristine, I don't feel it*; I don't see it. My response to you is, "Why not?" Who told you that you are not? Well they lied; you are beautiful. Beauty is not defined by makeup, hair lashes, or even what society says. You were made from greatness, love, and beauty because you are made in the image of God almighty. I want you to tell yourself three things about yourself that are beautiful beyond your physical features. See anyone can get made up, face contoured, hair done, and/or surgery to make things enhanced or to look "better." But take off these layers and tell me what you see? I see a strong girl/woman who won't quit. I see a girl/woman who has so much wisdom on the inside, a compassionate girl/woman, a person who is selfless, creative, multitalented, peaceful, honest, desired, needed, funny, and caring. Yep I see greatness in YOU! Now, I know you're like Kristine, you're not in my face. Well, if I were then that is what I would see and more. God didn't make any mess. He made you beautiful. You are a gift, a treasure, and the answer to what is needed. Don't think for one second that the negative comments others have said about you are true. You are precious, rare, uncommon, and a gem in God's chest. You are *His Priceless Jewel*. A great example of beauty is Queen Esther. She was chosen over all of the other beautiful women who were presented to the king. Her poise, her countenance, how she spoke to people, and her compassion for people are what captured the king's heart. I believe it was the God in her that drew him towards her. We, as women, must let our words and actions be full of love, authenticity, and compassion. For these are all attributes of beauty. What is on the inside reflects on the outside. When you open your mouth and speak, your expressions reveal all of the things that you really believe about yourself. Don't cover up with superficial things. Clothe yourself with wisdom, confidence, poise, compassion, and remember to sparkle and shine because after all, you are His treasured possession.

> DO THIS BECAUSE YOU ARE A PEOPLE SET APART AS HOLY TO GOD, YOUR GOD. GOD, YOUR GOD, CHOSE YOU OUT OF ALL THE PEOPLE ON EARTH FOR HIMSELF AS A CHERISHED, PERSONAL TREASURE.
> DEUTERONOMY 7:6

**Write down 3 things about yourself that are unique.**

I am unique because I can/have

_____

_____

_____

_____

I am unique because

_____

_____

_____

_____

I am unique because

_____

_____

_____

_____

Get up right now from where you are and go grab a mirror, look into the mirror and write down your thoughts on how you see yourself. Describe the "you" that you see behind closed doors. (For anything negative, I want you to look in the bible for what God says about you. For instance, if you perceive that you are not smart, you can read **Proverbs 14:1, Proverbs 31:18 Proverbs 31:26** for examples).

**Write down three things about yourself that are beautiful (outside of your physical attributes).**

I am beautiful because

_____

_____

_____

_____

I am beautiful because

_____

_____

_____

_____

I am beautiful because

_____

_____

_____

_____

Now take time over the next few days to ponder over what you wrote.

Remember **Psalms 139** shows us that you were sculpted, formed, and marvelously made. When God created you, He created a BEAUTIFUL WOMAN.

*Journal Notes*

_____
_____
_____
_____
_____
_____
_____
_____
_____
_____
_____
_____
_____
_____
_____
_____
_____
_____
_____

*A prayer for acceptance of your beauty:*

Father in the name of Jesus, I thank you that when I look into the mirror, I see what You see and that You created a woman who is marvelously made, confident, attractive, caring, compassionate, and wise. I am a woman after your own heart; therefore, I am healed from all past hurts, insecurities, and negative thinking.

I forgive _____ (call out all those who have hurt you) for hurting me and pray for their forgiveness and peace in their lives. My thoughts line up with Your thoughts and Your thoughts towards me are yes and Amen. I am accepted and loved by You. I am beautifully customized by Christ. In Jesus' name, AMEN.

## 02
### CHAPTER TWO

# God loves you this much...

For God so greatly loved and dearly prized the world that He (even) gave up His only begotten (unique) Son, so that whoever believes in (trusts in, clings to, relies on) Him shall not perish (come to destruction, be lost) but have eternal (everlasting) life.

John 3:16 (AMP)

But God- so rich is He in His mercy! Because of and in order to satisfy the great and wonderful and intense love with which he loved us.

Even when we were dead (slain) by [our own] shortcomings and trespasses, He made us alive together in fellowship and in union with Christ: [He gave us the very life of Christ Himself, the same new life with which He quickened Him, for] it is by grace (His favor and mercy which you did not deserve) that you are saved (delivered from judgement and made partakers of Christ's salvation).

And He raised us up together with Him and made us sit down together [giving us joint seating with Him] in the heavenly sphere [by virtue of our being]

in Christ Jesus (the Messiah, the Anointed One).

Ephesians 2: 4-6 (AMP)

What then shall we say to [all] this? If God is for us, who [can be] against us? [Who can be our foe, if God is on our side?]

Romans 8:31 (AMP)

As young women, we sometimes feel unloved and like no one cares for us. We often throw ourselves away because of mistakes we made that disappointed the ones we love. Often, these feelings are based on how someone else treats us or by what they do or don't do for us. We equate love with tangible gifts, compliments, or how often someone visits us or does things for us. Love has become so complex in this society that we often hear people say "if he loves you, he will do this" or "if you love me, you won't hurt me." Well, honestly, in these cases, if a person doesn't know how to love themselves then they can't love you and most importantly, if a person doesn't understand how much God loves them then they can't love you or receive love. Personally, I searched for love in so many ways—boys, friends, parties, and even clubbing. You say, clubbing, how does that make you loved? Well when I started getting noticed in the clubs in NYC and getting pulled from the red ropes and being asked to come straight to the VIP sections, I felt noticed, desired, and that is what I equated to love. Some of you know that feeling of walking into the hottest club and someone opening the door to decide who they will pull out of the line because they "fit" the look of the club. Well that was me and the people I ran with, the beautiful ones lol. We would walk up to certain places and no matter who the VIP was, we gained all access. I was on an all-time high. Woohoo they noticed me, look how hot we are, I received special treatment all night only to go home and return to my emptiness and rat race of trying to stay noticed.

After a while, the red rope privilege became boring; we made a name for ourselves—whoop-de-doo!! I was cute and dressed in the latest fashions, thanks to my cousin Tino who worked for the hottest lines in NYC. One night, I was even styled in Chanel. Guess who rocked the line that wasn't out yet? ME! This boosted me so much more because I had a name in the club scenes. People wanted to know who this model was. But I was still empty, still lonely, and still didn't know how to receive love. Some may say it's not that deep, but it really is. The crazy thing about all of this is that I was a born-again CHRISTIAN! Yet, the farther my eyes got off of the word, the further I sought the world to "make me someone" when God already said who I was.

At that place in my life, I knew the scripture said God loved me and I was created special, but it was not written on my heart. So, I went to the world to find someone to notice me and that meant I could make them love me once they got to know me. I wanted to feel cared for, needed, accepted, desired, and noticed. Ask yourself, honestly, why do you wear what you wear? I mean I like all the top designers on down to the unknowns, but sometimes, I would get dressed in certain clothes just to catch an eye or, as I would say, a compliment. I guess I am the only woman who had done this, NOT! It feels good to be complemented. Don't get me wrong, we are human, but it feels better when you know you're loved, know you're beautiful, and then someone compliments you out of pure regard. I needed to grasp that in Christ I am loved, needed, cared for, accepted, and desired. He needs me to show His light to others through my life. He cares for me because He sent His son to die for me.

# *I am accepted in Him because He created me.*

Well the understanding of His view of me, even though I read Jeremiah 29:11 quite often, didn't come until later in my life. In other words, it took time before I fully grasped how much He loves me and how beautiful I am.

What could have happened to me to make me feel the need to seek people's approval so much and the need to be loved you ask? Or maybe you didn't ask, but I am going to tell you. I believe it was when my mom passed away when I was 11. At times, I didn't understand fully what happened, but there was something missing. My mommy was gone. No more hugs, homemade birthday cakes, laughter, snuggling, or fun games together. No more watching wrestling at night when I was up past my bedtime just to be with her. My mom was everything to me. She was the one person who was always there. She was the comedy in our home and the music in our ears; she loved to surprise us and scare us. I mean there were days when I was in elementary school when she would keep me home just because. She felt that if I was doing great and my grades were up that I could just stay home and spend time with her. We would make something special to eat and just chill out together. She would make my favorite soup, split pea soup.

Looking back, I don't know how she made it, but while writing this, I can still smell and taste it. Sitting on the sofa, with hot soup, a toasted sandwich and my momma next to me was all this little girl needed. I loved and miss those days. It let me know how much she loved her kids and being with them. I was special, desired, noticed and appreciated. Holidays were times where she would go all out. Christmas was her favorite time of the year to celebrate Jesus and giving. For years, I fell for looking for St. Nicholas (the German name for Santa Claus). The house would be all normal: coffee table with two brown glass ashtrays and end tables with two brown glass bottom lamps with tan lampshades. Then all of a sudden, she would say "Kristina", yep she called me Kristina. "Go with your brother and sister and see if you can find St. Nicholas. I think I saw his lights outside and hear the bells on his sleigh." So, I would get my coat and rush outside with my sister and brother, going up the block and down the street looking in the sky for him. They would fake me out and say "oohh look over here, I see him" then I would look and see nothing, but stars. Then all of a sudden, they would chime in "I see him over the house." I would take off running to catch him. Once we got home, they would swear he was there. I would go inside and the whole house would be decorated—the railing would have garland, Christmas lights twinkled as I went up the stairs and the smell of fruit permeated the house. The coffee table would have St. Nicholas treys with almonds, walnuts, hazelnuts, and pecans. The other trays would have German chocolates, cookies, and a basket of oranges. I thought *there is no way mommy could have flipped this house this quickly.* He had to have come; she really knows him lol.

As I got older, I realized what she did and I even do it with my kids. My mom was super mom! With her being gone, I never grasped fully what her death meant. I just knew a huge hole was created in me—an emptiness, a longing. It seemed like overnight, my life went back to normal after she died. School started back and my dad went back to work, but my mommy wasn't there. I had no one to talk to, no one to snuggle with; my sister and brother were there, but no one could replace my mommy.

I was her baby girl. I knew she loved me. I felt like I was in a fog of confusion, like where did she go, where was love?

## As I got older, I began to search for affection and attention and didn't even realize it.

I wanted to be noticed like my mommy noticed me. This strong desire to be loved turned into my having relationship after relationship and once I got to high school, I was empty and didn't know it. Nothing or no one I met ever satisfied me. No drink, no man, no jewel, not even the hottest car made me happy. They just didn't give me what I was missing: the love, acceptance, and nurturing of a mother. I had my father growing up, but he was totally hurt and had major issues going on in his life. He did his best to protect us, instill in us to never give up, and that you have to make your own way, but no hugs, or words of affection. He always told us we were pretty not because of our hair or skin but because of who we are. For the most part, we spent 8 hours in school and came home to our father having to go to work on the night shift. So, in essence, I needed the nurturing of a mother and the approval of a father. Every daughter needs her mother's love and father's approval. I had missed this. It is not that my dad didn't want to show me, he just didn't know how. How many of you know or have heard that hurt people hurt other people? I realize now that my dad was so hurt and was void of love from his mother that he didn't know exactly how to express his love to us.

As I got older and really gave my heart to Christ, not just in words or church attendance, but really wanting more of Him in my life, I began to understand what REAL LOVE was! God's love is unconditional, meaning He loves us unconditionally. We do not have to perform for Him or buy things for Him. He just loves us just because. God's love is everlasting, meaning without end. His love never runs out or even wanes, but it's endless, so you can guarantee that after any mistake you make, His love is still there, no matter where you are in life. His love will outlast any and every one in your life.

GOD'S LOVE FOR US WILL REMAIN THE SAME. IT DOES NOT CHANGE BASED ON MOOD OR CIRCUMSTANCE. IT IS THE ONLY CONSTANT THING FLOWING IN YOUR LIFE THAT REMAINS UNINTERRUPTED. HIS LOVE IS ALWAYS PRESENT AND MORE THAN ENOUGH TO HEAL ANY SITUATION YOU HAVE COME OUT OF. I KNOW THIS BECAUSE I AM A LIVING WITNESS TO IT.

While living in NYC and doing life as the world says, I got pregnant by someone I barely knew, and at that moment I felt like "hey OK, God I hear ya." My whole life had changed. In a few seconds, conception took place. I felt like I disappointed God, my family, and myself. I was on the brink of having the modeling career I always wanted then I got pregnant. I had sex with no license and allowed someone who barely knew me to have access to something so precious. I went through so much (that story will be in a different book).

I was evicted from my apartment and my stuff was on the streets of NYC! I went to my boss and told her I was homeless. She was nice enough to give me money to get a hotel, my stuff out of storage, and a rental car to go back to Atlanta. The crazy thing is that I was homeless, pregnant, and walking the streets of NYC to find a hotel cheap enough to still have money left over to eat and get back home to Atlanta. It was midday and I was tired. About 10pm, I found a room near Times Square and rested there for the night. After about two days, I decided to head back home to Atlanta. During this whole time, I felt cut off from God and like I was a major disappointment. When I got home, I went to church and heard God's love yet again come from the pulpit. My sister and brother ministered to me and on a Sunday, I felt the confirmation that my child was not a mistake, but a blessing.

Regardless of the circumstance of their births, children are a heritage from God and a blessing. The bible doesn't say if you have one while married, it is a blessing (although this is the best scenario and I highly recommend it); it simply says God gave us gifts. Although my sin was premarital sex and a baby was created from that, it is God who gives life and I knew then my daughter had changed my life. I began to see how precious life was and how His unconditional love for me worked. Inside my womb was a blessing growing to teach me the Love of Jesus. From then on, I was on another level of growing more in grace. Through my daughter's eyes, I saw how God forgives us unlimitedly, how He fights for us, and how He sets us up to have the keys to the kingdom. My baby was a blessing that slowed me down from worldly living and wrong thinking. He tells us in His world in Hebrews 13:5 that He will never leave us nor forsake us. After all, He gave His only son up to die for you and me! Do you know anyone who would do that? How much love is it to sacrifice your only son for the sake of saving others, others who do not know you, others who may not even talk to you, others who will make mistakes and sometimes ignore you? That is a love that outweighs your faults, your moods, your lack of praying, and your attitude. It's a love that moves mountains and heals souls. This love that God has for you is far beyond your imagination.

How many people do you know who would chase you down in the midst of your wrong just to say, "Hey, I love you and I am still here for you?" That is what Jesus does for us daily. Look at Matthew 13:45-46: "Again, the kingdom of heaven is like a merchant seeking fine pearls, and upon finding one pearl of great value, he went and sold all that he had and bought it." You see here that God gave up His precious son, Jesus, for us, the valued prize; we are His beloved. In Ezekiel 34:11, we see these words: "For thus says the Lord God: Behold, I myself will search for My sheep and seek them out." When we look at this comparison, I am in awe because sheep tend to stray; they get lost and often do silly things but God, as our shepherd, seeks us out and protects us when we stray. He brings us back home with an arm of love. How great is that to see His love for us. This clearly shows us not to look to man or things to fill your Love tank, but to look to God after all. He sent His one and only son to die for you. Yes, YOU!!! He chose you before he formed the world; you were on His mind, now that is LOVE!!!

**Take the time to reflect on the little things God has done for you in His constant acts of love. Write those love nuggets here:**

_____
_____
_____
_____
_____
_____
_____
_____
_____
_____

There is nothing that God would not do for you. There is nothing he would withhold. That is love. Psalms 84:11 says "for the Lord God is our own sun and our shield. He gives us grace and glory. The Lord will withhold no good thing from those who do what is right."

Have confidence in His LOVE because He is always there with you, no matter what mistakes you may make or have made. He will never leave you.

> THEY'LL GET TO KNOW ME BY BEING KINDLY FORGIVEN, WITH THE SLATE OF THEIR SINS FOREVER WIPED CLEAN.
>
> HEBREWS 8:12 (MSG)

**Find someone you can show random acts of love towards.**

1. Write down how it made you feel doing it.

_____
_____
_____
_____
_____
_____
_____
_____

2. What was their response?

_____
_____
_____
_____
_____
_____
_____
_____

## 03
**CHAPTER THREE**

# Never Give Up

I have strength for all things in Christ who empowers me [I am ready for anything equal to anything through Him Who infuses inner strength into me; I am self-sufficient in Christ sufficiency].

Philippians 4:13 (AMP)

Be strong, courageous and firm; fear not nor be in terror before them, for it is the Lord your God who goes with you, He will not fail you or forsake you.

Deuteronomy 31:6

The Lord is my strength and my [impenetrable] Shield, my heart trusts in, relies on, and confidently leans on Him, and I am helped; therefore, my heart greatly rejoices and with my song, I will praise Him.

Psalm 28:7 (AMP)

But those who wait for the Lord [who expect, look for, and hope in Him] shall change and renew their strength and power, they shall lift their wings and mount up [close to God] as eagles [mount up to the sun]

Isaiah 40:31

As you see in these love notes from God, He is always encouraging you. It is like a cheerleader on the sidelines of a football game, rooting for you, and cheering for you to keep you encouraged. When times get tough, don't look at the circumstances; instead, look inside of you, think back on other areas of your life that were hard and see how you overcame them. Reflect on how you accomplished something you once doubted. If God helped you before, He will do it again, and again and again.

In life, we are faced with decisions, obstacles, and storms of all sorts, but with God, we always have a way to escape and overcome. Anything you set your mind to, you can and will accomplish it because God is on the inside of you and in Him there is no failure!

He is your strength when you are weak. Just ask Him to help, like you would ask your parents, teachers, or friends. After all, He created you and this entire world. He knows it all; don't let others break your confidence. People only call other people names because of their own insecurities and hurts. Pray for those who attack you and ask God to step in and give you strength.

I recall when I got pregnant again after my second daughter was born in 2011, there was something that just didn't seem right. As a mom, you know by instinct certain things about your body (or, shall I say, you should know). I had experienced a blighted ovum in the first year of my marriage in 2008 that was devastating to me. We were in our third month, and I just wasn't comfortable with my doctor at the time. My husband's co-workers recommended the company's OB-GYN, so we went in to see him. I will never forget, as the appointment went forward and after formally meeting him and his getting to know my history, he moved us to the ultrasound room. Within minutes, he noticed something that didn't look correct. He called a nurse in the room; this is when time seemed to stand still, and the nurse confirmed there was no baby in the sac.

He was so apologetic and comforting, assuring us it was nothing we did. Now, this was within my first six months of being married. My husband and oldest daughter were in the room. I began to weep, and all I could think was, "Will I ever have another child"? Will I ever give my husband a son? As we went back home, I felt defeated and like I was not a full woman. My mind was an open battlefield for the enemy as thoughts came in by the dozen. I began to read about blighted ovums, the D&C surgery and how there were several instances where a D&C was performed and the baby showed up. I found the scripture in the bible in Ezekiel 37:6 NLT which says "I will put breath into you, and you will come to life, vs 7 so I spoke this message, just as he told me. Suddenly as I spoke, there was a rattling noise all across the valley. The bones of each body came together and attached themselves as a complete skeletons vs 8 Then as I watched muscles and flesh formed over the bones. Then skin formed to cover their bodies. They all came to life and stood up on their feet- a great army" this was the scripture that I stood on, hoping that my baby would show up.

I saw it and quoted it. Well after two weeks, still no baby. Was I disappointed? Yes, but I knew that this would be oK. It had to be, why else would I see that scripture. I honestly felt like I threw a blanket on a problem and expected it to work. I know the word works, but was my faith there to see manifestation? I knew that baby wasn't there. After my surgery, I recovered so quickly and without any problems. I waited a few months and we decided to seek the fertility doctor and make sure all was well with the both of us. During our appointment that was so intrusive, I felt like man. We had to do all of this: have sex, take a temperature, and go back to the doctor the day after having sex to get checked. And then go when we don't have sex, test this, scrape that. For WHATT????

Now, for some women, this is what you had to do to make sure all was right even before you conceived, but for ME—and I do say ME and my household—that was not the direction God had planned for us. Our doctor was like there is really no issue; it will happen in time. The funny thing was each time we were to have sex and go to the doctor to get checked, Mike was out of town!!! So yeah after two months of taking my temperature and planning sex, I was over sex.

I didn't want to feel like an appointment had to be made to enjoy my husband. I began to see in the bible that each time a woman laid with a man, even in the time of Noah, the woman conceived. There were so many examples of times where "she laid with him and conceived" or "at the appointed season, she conceived" so I told my husband I didn't think it took all of that testing and temperature monitoring. When I lay with you in love and enjoyment, we shall conceive! Well months later, my husband came home from traveling and we had a few minutes of being intimate before he left again. I laid with him and conceived!!! I didn't even know I was pregnant. A few weeks later, I had a cough and a cold. I wasn't feeling well. I had a high fever, sore throat etc. Mike took me to the ER. They said that I might be pregnant, but the sinus infection had to be treated. The doctor didn't want to give me antibiotics; he wanted the cold to run its course. After a few minutes of discussing the possibility of my being pregnant and my past history of sinus infections, he decided to give me a pregnancy test. Minutes later, it was positive.

Throughout all of this—the doubts that came that I would never conceive or get pregnant with my second daughter—God kept me. I had my fears in the beginning, and some of the tests for the baby were showing abnormal, but God, she was perfect! Now, here we were in 2012, pregnant again, and this time, something just didn't feel right. I thought it was fear from my 2008 experience, so I shunned it, prayed, confessed, and just kept moving as best as I could. Thoughts like "our baby is not growing" would come and go. I would imagine that as I would go see my doctor, she would say "there is no baby here" so I went to my appointments to see how far along I was and to check on the baby. Sure enough, it was in there and cute as could be, just a little pea in the pod. So, with me being the pregnancy and kid junkie that I was, I wanted to hear the heartbeat. I knew it was early, but I was just so eager to hear that lovely whoosh sound. As she put on the monitor and we heard a slow heartbeat, I knew something wasn't right. We checked it again and the beats were too slow. My doctors advised me to check back within a couple of weeks to see how the baby's progress was before we started thinking anything.

My next appointment was the week of Christmas, and low and behold, there was no heartbeat. Looking at the baby on the sonogram in a slumped position just wrecked me. I felt like I couldn't help him. I wept and went home. As I stood in my kitchen, I knew we had bible study that night. I began to cry and my husband noticed. I cried out "I'm sorry that I haven't given you a son yet. I am sorry this happened". See I grew up hearing that it was an honor to give your husband a male seed. Can we say BONDAGE!!! I now know that any child you give to your husband, or have in your family, male or female, is a blessing from GOD!

Everything that I felt was real; the feeling that something wasn't right was correct. After that moment of my bursting out to my husband, he began to minister to me (talk about being thankful for a man after God's own heart). I was no longer hurt because

God's sustaining grace had covered me and out of that came a pregnancy confession CD. We went to bible study as if this didn't happen. Not that we were ignoring it, but that God had me and has me; I felt a peace, so I moved forward. It was weird because my crying time was about 30 minutes. I got my thoughts out; my husband gave the word; and we moved forward. I know this was God's sustaining grace. Only He can help you when pain is that deep. One person we told at church was like why are you here at bible study? I said why not, what am I going to do at home? I can't cry anymore. I felt like there was this shield over me or this blanket covering me and my thoughts.

I had to force myself to think about what happened, like really force myself to meditate on my child going to heaven. Even then a tear would form but not fall. There was a weird joy that overcame me, peace, calm, and a comfort in knowing that all was well. In that moment, I knew He had me and His grace became more real to me. I had the surgery and moved forward. But how many of you know when you think you passed a test, a presentation will come. Well my test came again in 2013. I conceived again, and this time, the battle was real. My mind was attacked with all that went wrong the other times vs the fact that I had two other healthy children. Each appointment for me was anxiety central. I felt peace, but my mind was in negativeville. I remember having images of no baby or a miscarriage, and when I didn't feel the baby move, I would panic. Then, one day while showering, I heard loud and clear like someone was in the room with me, "BLESSED IS THE FRUIT OF YOUR WOMB" I was like "Yeah, I am blessed" Then, I heard it again, but this time a question followed, "What is blessed?"

> *Favored, strong, healthy, and empowered to prosper.*

Hmmm, so if my womb is blessed and is a part of me, I am blessed. My baby is blessed, and the environment my baby is in is blessed. I began to praise God, and when I did I heard, "This baby will be fine". As I went to my next appointment to see the sex and how the growth was, I saw my handsome son on the screen! Strong and perfect! My battle still continued because now it was a mind-renewal process. I had a word from God, but I still had days where I would doubt. I had to constantly change the way I thought. When women would approach me with their sad pregnancy and delivery stories, I had to just smile and speak the word. I remember one day having to go to the Labor and Delivery Unit because we thought the fluid was leaking from my sac. My husband had to remind me of what I shared with Him that God told me and also remind me of how great and awesome God is to us. As we were tested and the doctors and nurses were prepping me in the event that I had to deliver, I was about to freak out because I was thinking: "He is too young, now is not the time," then I remembered

my confessions. God reminded me that BLESSED is the FRUIT of MY WOMB and THIS BABY SHALL BE FINE. Needless to say, we went home several hours later.

When the month of my delivery arrived, I began to have intensified thoughts of a bad delivery, that my baby wouldn't make it or that something complicated would take place. I had to fight those thoughts with every fiber of my being. Let me say this, not only was my entire pregnancy smooth, but my delivery was super smooth. So much so that I was pushing and paused to laugh at something when my son wiggled himself out sunny side up! The moment I held him was so awesome. As they cleaned him up, I heard God remind me of this, "I told you this baby shall be fine. Look around and see how much I love you". I began to weep. He did it, and He protected me and gave me my son effortlessly.

What I have shared is a light version of what I went through mentally. But I wanted to show you that no matter how tough situations get, stay focused on God's love, and when the days are rough, just worship and thank Him. When the days are still and calm, thank Him even more. NO matter how hard it gets, how rough it seems, or how long it takes, what God has promised you will come to pass. I am a living witness. Do not allow the negative thoughts from the enemy to reside in your mind for one second. When the thought of failure comes, remind yourself of who you are and there is no failure in Jesus. When someone says you'll never succeed, stick to the plan that was set before you.

Failures don't come through trying; they come when you do not try at all. When all of the walls of life are caving in, remind yourself of the times that he has pushed the walls back and down so you can make it through. No matter how small the situation or how different the breakthrough, it is part of God's track record of always being there for you.

> *In life, we are faced with decisions, obstacles, and storms of all kinds, but with God, we always have a way of escape.*

Anything you set your mind to you can and will accomplish because God is on the inside of you and in Him there is no failure. He is your strength when you are weak, so just ask Him to help like you would ask your parents, teacher or friends. After all, He created you and this entire world; He knows it all. Don't let others affect how you feel. People only call other people names because of their own insecurities and hurt. Pray for those who attack you and ask God to step in and give you strength. DO NOT QUIT, it is not an option! HUGS!!!

# God's Love Note

Is there any god like God?
Are we not at bedrock?
Is not this the God who armed me,
then aimed me in the right direction?
Now I run like a deer;
I'm king of the mountain.
He shows me how to fight;
I can bend a bronze bow!
You protect me with salvation-armor;
you hold me up with a firm hand,
caress me with your gentle ways.
You cleared the ground under me
so my footing was firm.
When I chased my enemies I caught them;
I didn't let go till they were dead men.
I nailed them; they were down for good;
then I walked all over them.
You armed me well for this fight,
you smashed the upstarts.
You made my enemies turn tail,
and I wiped out the haters.
They cried "uncle"
but Uncle didn't come;
They yelled for God
and got no for an answer.
I ground them to dust; they gusted in the wind.
I threw them out, like garbage in the gutter.

**Psalm 18:31-42 (MSG)**

**Take time to write down 2 instances when you wanted to quit and how God helped you through. Write down the thoughts you had and then share what took place. See how your negative thoughts and what God did don't match; God will never do anything to harm you.**

_____

_____

_____

_____

_____

_____

_____

_____

_____

_____

_____

_____

_____

_____

_____

_____

_____

_____

04
CHAPTER FOUR

# Confidence

## con·fi·dence (noun)

*the feeling or belief that one can rely on someone or something; firm trust.*

For the Lord shall be your confidence, firm and strong, and shall keep your foot from being caught [in a trap or some hidden danger].

Proverbs 3:26 (AMP)

_____
_____
_____
_____
_____
_____
_____
_____
_____
_____
_____

**When do you believe you are most confident?**

When doubt tries to come, in any area, focus on God's word for you and you will get through it.

As a young woman, there are many areas where your confidence can be attacked: physical appearance, school, work, talents, friendship, and relationships. Often, the struggle is because of an uncertainty of who you are or whose you are. You may begin to ask yourself questions like am I good at this, am I really pretty and the list goes on and on. Well, let me tell you, Priceless Jewel, you are the daughter of THE KING! Yep, that's right, you are royalty! You are more than what you see. There is so much depth to you and so much wisdom inside of you.

## Reflect with me for a minute.

If your dad is the king, and you're his Princess, is there anything you don't have access to? Is there anything you can ask for and not receive? Is there lack in your life? NO! As God's Princess, you have access to the entire kingdom. All you have to do is ask: "Father, help me to be confident in the areas of _____ and _____. Lord show me how to accomplish _____." You have the right to get help in any area of your life, even as a believer. God is there to meet all of your needs, just like the king provides for his Princess.

## Be who God created you to be, take that crown out of your pocket and place it on your head.

Confidence comes from a place of being genuine and original. Knowing who you are in Him brings confidence because no one can tell you differently. The only true way to know who you are and gain that confidence is to get in His word. You must open your bible and begin to see how He sees you. A princess doesn't walk around with her head down or is ashamed of what she wears or who doesn't like her. She is not moved by those OUTSIDE of the KINGDOM! She knows that she is beautiful in the King's eyes and beyond physical beauty which can fade or be scared. He accepts everything about her. Only the love of the King moves her.

By definition, confidence is "a belief, a feeling, a firm trust". Ask yourself: Who or what do you trust the most? Is it your beauty, which can fade, how well you dress, the feeling of walking in stiletto heels, when someone compliments you, when your hair is done, rocking a designer handbag, or is it knowing that you are created and chosen by Almighty God himself?

When an athlete is picked in the first round of a draft or a beauty contestant is picked to be Miss. America, there is a firm confidence well before they are chosen that this is who they are and who they were created to be. Yes, sometimes, there may be brief periods of doubt from time to time, based on circumstances, but when you know that you are designed by the very hand of God, there should be a pep in your step that pushes you beyond what others may negatively say about you. It's like that feeling you get when you know something is yours or supposed to go your way. Well that is the confidence I am talking about— knowing that you are greater, that you deserve better, and that you should have more.

As women, we are always put in boxes that say that beauty, fashion, extensions, and a made-up face with the right outfit can give us confidence. I disagree! Now, don't get me wrong, I know firsthand wearing a sharp pencil skirt with a bad top and some hot shoes can make you feel good superficially, but when you take all of that off, do you feel the same? If you had on rags, would you feel the same? Probably not. See, confidence has to be a mindset, knowing that I am who I am and I do not have to be like anyone else. We allow others to compare us to all these photoshopped pictures of women, who, for the most part, are wearing hair, eyelashes, nails, and clothes that don't belong to them. We have to appreciate how God designed us.

I don't look like my neighbor; I am not built like my neighbor. I am different, and I know I am special. There is no one else like me in the world, no one who walks like me, talks like me, or acts like me. Be firm in who you are and believe that you are beautiful, whether you have short hair, long hair, thick hair or no hair. Believe that you are unique, tall, short, thick, or thin. Believe that you are who God created you to be and accept yourself—remember, God did.

Reading Luke 12?7 makes me think about how much God knows about us, how he intimately knows us, and accepts us. I recall when dating I wanted these men to love me, know me, and care so deeply about me. When all along, they only wanted one thing. Being a King's daughter, I knew He knew how to love me, accept me, and affirm me. I was so busy looking for love and love was always right there. I mean think about it, when dating some guys, they only know the information you tell them. They don't know anything about your past, your heart's desire, what you aspire to be or intimate thoughts unless they dig deep enough to find out. And often, if you don't tell, they aren't asking. I mean, yeah, some will ask because they are generally interested in you and want to know more. The picture that I am trying to paint is that they need to grow to that deep intimate side where you share your heart. In the meantime, you have a Father who has your heart. He loves you regardless of if you call twice a day, once a week, or never and He isn't looking for anything in return for His love. He doesn't need you to prove yourself or your love to Him; He just asks that you trust and believe in Him. Being confident that God has you can allow you to feel free to be who you are in any relationship without jumping through hoops to keep someone.

*You are altogether beautiful, my love; there is no flaw in you.*

SONG OF SOLOMON 4:7

**Read the book of Esther and see how a normal girl was chosen to be Queen.**

## Things to ponder:

What was it that drew the King to Esther?

_____
_____
_____
_____
_____
_____

What made her confident to go before the King?

_____
_____
_____
_____
_____
_____
_____

# In what areas in your life do you lack confidence?

**Take a day when you can grab a pen and paper, find a comfy space, and go before God and ask Him how he sees you. Ask Him to reveal the areas of your life that lack confidence. Then, allow Him to heal you in those areas and watch how you flourish.**

What areas are you going to work on?

_____

_____

_____

_____

_____

_____

_____

_____

_____

_____

_____

_____

_____

_____

_____

SHE IS VALU[ABLE]
SHE IS PRICELESS
HER HUSBAND
SHE COMFORTS A[ND]
SHE IS FILLED WI[TH]
SHE IS STRONG  SHE IS F[AITHFUL]
SHE SPEAKS
SHE DISPLAYS DIGNITY  [S]HE
SHE HONORS GOD

THE PROVERBS 31 WOMAN

BLE

TRUST IN HER

ENCOURAGES

TREASURE

USED   SHE IS FEARLESS

KIND WORDS

CHILDREN CALL HER BLESSED

D HE PRAISES HER

05
CHAPTER FIVE

# The Priceless Jewel
## Description of a Worthy Woman

A good woman is hard to find,
and worth far more than diamonds.
Her husband trusts her without reserve, and never has reason to regret it.
Never spiteful, she treats him generously all her life long.
She shops around for the best yarns and cottons, and enjoys knitting and sewing.
She's like a trading ship that sails to faraway places and brings back exotic surprises.
She's up before dawn, preparing breakfast for her family and organizing her day.
She looks over a field and buys it, then, with money she's put aside, plants a garden.
First thing in the morning, she dresses for work, rolls up her sleeves, eager to get started.
She senses the worth of her work, is in no hurry to call it quits for the day.
She's skilled in the crafts of home and heart, diligent in homemaking.
She's quick to assist anyone in need, reaches out to help the poor.
She doesn't worry about her family when it snows; their winter clothes are all mended and ready to wear.
She makes her own clothing, and dresses in colorful linens and silks. Her husband is greatly respected when he deliberates with the city fathers.
She designs gowns and sells them, brings the sweaters she knits to the dress shops.
Her clothes are well-made and elegant, and she always faces tomorrow with a smile.
When she speaks she has something worthwhile to say, and she always says it kindly.
She keeps an eye on everyone in her household, and keeps them all busy and productive.
Her children respect and bless her; her husband joins in with words of praise:
"Many women have done wonderful things, but you've outclassed them all!"
Charm can mislead and beauty soon fades. The woman to be admired and praised is the woman who lives in the Fear-of-God.
Give her everything she deserves! Festoon her life with praises!

Proverbs 31 (MSG)

Let not yours be the [merely] external adorning with [elaborate] interweaving and knotting of the hair, the wearing of jewelry, or changes of clothes.

1 Peter 3:3

As with the definition of Priceless and Jewel, in the beginning of the book, we see that a Priceless Jewel is someone whose value cannot be determined. She is treasured, rare, and hard to find. Are you rare and hard to find, or do you fit the mode of every other girl? Some of the greatest examples of a young lady like this are found in Proverbs 31, 1 Peter 3:3, and the book of Esther, just to name a few. All of these examples are young women who seek God first and in all that they do. As a young woman, it is rare to find a young woman study the word and clothe herself in strength and dignity (Proverbs 31:21). We usually want to wear what the trend is or what we think will impress others. The women mentioned here were more concerned with what God thought than what others had to say.

This is a very safe place to be because God will never let you down. His thoughts toward us are always good, no matter what we are or how our hair looks. Reflect on this:

## God's Love Note

FOR I KNOW THE THOUGHTS AND PLANS THAT I HAVE FOR YOU, SAYS THE LORD, THOUGHTS AND PLANS FOR WELFARE AND PEACE AND NOT FOR EVIL, TO GIVE YOU HOPE IN YOUR FINAL OUTCOME.
JEREMIAH 29:11

I never saw myself as a Priceless Jewel, rare, unique or hard to find. I was so hurt deep down inside that I began to internalize this negative, tough girl attitude about myself. I wouldn't let too many people close to me, and when I did, I didn't trust them. I felt like everyone was out for something and never giving me anything but a hurt heart. Growing up, I kept hearing how special I was, and how pretty and smart I was, but I didn't feel very special, pretty or smart. I mean, why was I special? I got into a lot of trouble, I was often mean to protect myself from being hurt or I was overly nice to accommodate others. But I was never really me. As I think back, who was I anyway?

When I got older and had my daughter, Kloe, I began to see how much God loved me. When I had her in my late 20s, I saw firsthand how much God loved me. I saw it through my daughter's eyes, seeing her form in my womb, hearing her heart beat, and delivering her. Having my daughter and learning how it felt to love someone so much, I began to see God's love. Years later, my husband showed me something I will never forget in Ephesians 2. I had read this before and I'd seen it in church also. This time, my husband took his time to share how God made me alive when I was dead in my sin and that He was so rich in His mercy that he gave us a wonderful and intense love by giving us Christ; this showed me just how priceless I was. It showed me that I am everything the Proverbs 31 woman says I am. I am everything God says I am- beautiful, wonderfully made, chosen, and sculpted. It did not matter what mistakes I had made because He saw them from the beginning before He created me. God knew I would make mistakes. He knew I would bear a child out of wedlock; He knew and He still loves me. I am a Priceless Jewel because I am His handiwork. In Him, I am all that and more, mistakes and all!

Let's look at the Proverbs 31 woman:

(v10-31) She was a young woman who was never spiteful, (v12-13) but she was a crafty business woman. She spent time with God before she did anything else (15) and she was a thinker, considering things before she moved on them (v16). She assisted the poor; (v20) she was caring, had confidence in God and didn't worry about stormy weather [tough times]. (v21) She was a young woman who wore strength and dignity (vs25) and she spoke kind words and words of wisdom. (v26) She worshiped and feared the Lord; (30) she was a Priceless Jewel rare, not like any other woman. She didn't conform to the pressures of her female peers, but she did what she liked and what the Lord approved of for her life. She was neither boastful nor rude; she didn't have to fit in.

This Priceless Jewel just served God, and He showed her how to do anything she needed. Be Priceless—rare, different, uncommon. Be a Jewel—polished, treasured and sought after. Be YOU!

# Things to ponder:

**What about the Proverbs 31 woman do you want to see in your life?**

_____
_____
_____
_____
_____
_____
_____
_____
_____
_____
_____
_____
_____
_____
_____

**Read Psalms 139 and see how God is concerned about your every detail.**

**This is a scripture that you can actually meditate on daily to see how God knows who you are; he knows when you are resting; and he knows when you rise. He is always around you.**

What are some of the advantages of someone knowing so much about you and caring about everything you do? Even if you make mistakes, is God still near? Do you sense God in your day?

_____

_____

_____

_____

_____

_____

_____

_____

_____

_____

_____

_____

_____

_____

_____

_____

06
CHAPTER SIX

# Beauty From the Inside Out

Let not yours be the [merely] external adorning with [elaborate] interweaving and knotting of the hair, the wearing of jewelry, or changes of clothes;

But let it be the inward adorning and beauty of the hidden person of the heart, with the incorruptible and unfading charm of a gentle and peaceful spirit, which [is not anxious or wrought up, but] is very precious in the sight of God.

1 Peter 3:3-4 (AMPC)

_____
_____
_____
_____
_____
_____
_____
_____
_____
_____
_____
_____
_____

When we think of beauty, we think of hair, nails, skin complexion, clothes, makeup, etc., but do we ever think of the heart or the spirit of a young woman? We all know that our hair will one day turn grey, our skin may sag or wrinkle, our clothes may not fit or we may begin to look different in some way; we won't look exactly like we did when we were teenagers, but our spirit- the real us- will never fade or go out of style. Don't get me wrong; there is nothing wrong with doing your hair or wearing makeup. Heck, I love me some makeup products, lipsticks, highlighter for my cheeks and a bad pair of stilettos, but that does not make me who I am.

MY INNER BEAUTY IS THE QUIETNESS OF MY SPIRIT, MY KIND WORDS TO OTHERS; THE LOVE I HAVE FOR JESUS; HOW I HONOR HIM NOT ONLY AT CHURCH, BUT AT HOME, SCHOOL, WORK, THE MALL, OR WHEN I AM AT A FRIEND'S HOUSE; IT IS HOW I HONOR MY PARENTS AND TEACHERS.

These are things that matter. These qualities capture what real beauty is. See, you can paint your face, dress up your anger, nasty attitude and style your hair but when you open your mouth, the real you comes out. What's deep down inside always comes to the surface when pressure is applied or when things linger there long enough. When you open your mouth, is it beauty or is it ugly that they see? What is inside of you will always reflect on the outside.

Spending time in the Word, reading His love letters to you, pondering on His thoughts and His plan for you, will create an inner beauty that will enhance what is on the outside. I thought for so long that my long hair (at the time before I cut it) and my being tall and thin would be enough, but as I came to learn, that wasn't the case. One day, when I was applying for a modeling job, the interviewer began to just chit chat because he knew my stylist friend who referred me. So, we were having a conversation, and the real me came out when he asked if I was willing to work certain shows at low rates. I had this attitude that everyone owed me, and it was obvious. He didn't want to work with me at all, not because I wasn't tall enough or pretty enough but because my attitude was not what he wanted on his set. I began to notice that it wasn't about my outer beauty, but about who I was on the inside, specifically, the person I saw in the mirror and heard in my private thoughts when I was all alone. And who I was on the inside was not pretty but ugly on so many levels; I knew God but didn't see myself as He saw me.

Learning to focus on God and learning how to love others and love myself brought a change to my outer appearance and to my spirit. This is what made me beautiful. I took a look at Queen Esther and saw how she carried herself with such respect and honor, how she sought God in all that she did and how she obeyed God no matter what the circumstance. It was not her outer beauty that grabbed the King, as he had so many beautiful women to choose from. I believe she was beautiful inside and out, and her confidence and obedience to God moved the King to desire her above all.

## For my school girls, here is a challenge

For my younger readers, wear a uniform style outfit for one week. Light top and tan bottoms or dark top and tan bottoms—something plain and generic, with no color or glitter. If you're in private school, maybe wear your hair in a bun or simple and plain. If you already do this, wear no makeup and if you don't wear makeup and wear your hair in a bun then I challenge you to do something you normally wouldn't do. Go meet someone you have never met in school and/or sit with someone different at lunch.

## Here is another challenge

Offer help to your teacher or parent in an area you normally don't help in. Do this for a week without being asked to. Say a kind word to your parents each day, and to a classmate who you never talk to. Later in this section, you will have a chance to journal how you felt in a uniform, what your thoughts were, and what people said.

For my grown-ups, you must do the opposite of what you typically do, if you dress to the 9s all the time, you must dress down in natural colors—tan, creams or just wear a white shirt and light pants for a week. If you wear makeup, do not wear make-up this week—just some gloss. If you don't wear make-up, try something different, go to a make-up counter and get some help in this area. Wear simple, clean hair styles. At the end of this week, I want you to look over your journal and determine if your cute outfits and accessories are more powerful than kind and loving acts of the heart. If being confident in who you are matters more than your outward appearance or if your inward beauty will shine brighter than the outward appearance, you may need to work on your inward beauty and that is fine—I did.

JOURNAL DAY 1

JOURNAL DAY 2

JOURNAL DAY 3

JOURNAL DAY 4

JOURNAL DAY 5

JOURNAL DAY 6

JOURNAL DAY 7

**How do you feel after this week of reflection?**

07
**CHAPTER SEVEN**

# The Greatest Fashion
## What attitude do you wear?

And you shall love the Lord your God out of and with your whole heart and out of and with all your life and out of and with all your mind (with your faculty of thought and your moral understanding) and out of and with all your strength. This is the first and principal commandment.

Mark 12:30 (AMP)

# love

Love is the greatest outfit you can wear. After all, love is not selfish, self-centered, haughty, or mean. When you put God first in all that you do, your automatic response to everything will be love. If you show love toward everyone in your life and in everything you do, you will have the greatest outcome in every situation. As women, we tend to wear our emotions on our faces, or in our tone of voice toward others or situations. This can often lead to someone prejudging us based on the attitude we "wear" or display.

I recall starting a job, and everyone there thought I was just mean, rude, and curt. Really, I was just quiet and not talking very much because I didn't know anyone. But when someone would question me, I would get defensive, as if I had something to prove. The attitude outfit I had on was not a positive one. I had to realize that what I presented was neither nice nor peaceful. I went into the position feeling like I had to prove myself because I didn't have a degree or a lot of experience. I was hired anyway, so that alone should have told me I was "qualified."

Over the course of a few weeks, I got to know one of the ladies there, and she began to see a different attitude (outfit). She saw the real me and admitted that everyone had it all wrong. She shared with me that I didn't have to be defensive, but just confident in who I am. The funny thing is I was thinking: You have to be confident in who you are, well what if I don't believe in myself or quite know who I am, then where does my confidence come from? Without a foundation in God, how do I discover myself? I had to take a long hard look at myself and say "who am I"?

## Why do I respond the way that I do?

Most of the time, it's me trying to prove myself or make myself be seen. It comes from a defensive posture or from a position of hurt, disrespect, and/or lack of attention. I was beat down inside, so my attitude outside was not always nice. Starting a new job, joining a new school, being married, and getting to know new family members can challenge you to "prove" yourself when you are not confident in whose you are. Well, when we are resting in who Jesus designed us to be, we can be sure that He already accepted us before the foundation of the world. When I know I am loved and valued, my whole demeanor will change and so will yours. Trust me, you won't show up at work trying to prove how smart you are, or prove your idea will work.

You will submit to leadership and flow with your portion. (The submission topic is a whole new book with limitless topics, so I won't touch on that right now). Once I really looked at myself and reflected on my co-worker's words, I took them to heart, and from that point on, I began to dress my attitude differently. I don't act a certain way towards people because of how they act towards me; I treat them like I want to be treated, regardless. So, I choose to wear love.

You may ask, "How does a person wear love?' Love is visible, just like your t-shirt, jeans, or shoes. Even if you have a bad attitude, it is visible. What is in your heart is always on display. I challenge you to boldly wear the most fashionable outfit, carved out of the most exquisite material—love. It goes with any situation you can come up against. With hurt, there is forgiveness, which is rooted in love. With gossip, there is loyalty, which is also rooted in love. The antidote to anger is understanding, which is also rooted in love, and complaining is counteracted with patience, again rooted in love.

See there are many examples of love being found in all things. After all, love never fails, fades, or goes out of style. Wear it well and reap the harvest of its constantly flowing fruit. Jesus is the best example of love. He gave His life for you, well before you were born, formed in your mother's womb, or before your parents were formed. He never quits on you. He is always there and always forgives. That is LOVE!

# Things to ponder:

Starting today, what are some love accessories you can wear?

_____
_____
_____
_____
_____
_____

How can you adorn yourself with love differently each day?

_____
_____
_____
_____
_____
_____
_____

What areas in your life do you feel need a wardrobe change?

## 08
CHAPTER EIGHT

# Be Bold

## bōld (adjective)

*(of a person, action, or idea) showing an ability to take risks; confident and courageous.*

*(of a color or design) having a strong or vivid appearance.*

The wicked flee when no man pursues them, but the [uncompromisingly] righteous are bold as a lion.

Proverbs 28:1 (AMP)

For God did not give us a spirit of timidity (of cowardice, of craven and cringing and fawning fear) but [He has given us a spirit] of power and of love and of calm and well-balanced mind and discipline and self- control.

2 Timothy 1:17

For this reason, since the day we heard about you, we have not stopped praying for you. We continually ask God to fill you with the knowledge of his will through all the wisdom and understanding that the spirit gives so that you may live a life worthy of the Lord and please him in every way: bearing fruit in every good work, growing in the knowledge of God, being strengthened with all power according to his glorious might so that you may have great endurance and patience.

Colossians 1:9-11

Esther, who went into the presence of a King without being summoned, was BOLD. She knew the risk was great; yet, she heard from God and was confident in what she was doing.

Luke 1:26-33 Amplified Bible (AMP)

Confident, courageous and strong...I remember when I was in high school and people would say that being bold was for those girls who would talk back to teachers or get loud with students in the classroom. They would be the ones who would snap on people at the drop of a hat, being loud, boisterous, and always drawing attention to themselves. They would say, "She's bold!" Well, as a Priceless Jewel, that is not the kind of bold we want to be. That is rude and ignorant behavior. The boldness I am speaking of is a quiet confidence, an assertiveness that is strong in the decisions we make. We spend time in the Word, and we are able to see who we are in Him. We don't have to be loud and rude to people nor do we have to be seen to gain respect or feel strong. I know it is hard when someone is rude or disrespectful to you and you want to let them know a thing or two. To that, my question is: What is the benefit of getting back at them with rudeness? What does it do for you to sink to their level of ignorance? In reacting this way, you have just given in. As Priceless Jewels, we can intelligently handle situations. There should never be a time that someone draws you out of character. We are strong because Jesus is on the inside of us!

Mary was a great example of a BOLD woman, not only for being a virgin in her day, but for being the Mother of Christ, having never laid with her husband Joseph and becoming pregnant. She was bold by standing on what God told her, no matter what the consequence.

The woman with the issue of blood was BOLD; she knew the consequences of her going into public. No matter the cost, she knew that she was taking a great risk.

# Jesus' Birth Foretold

[26] Now in the sixth month [of Elizabeth's pregnancy] the angel Gabriel was sent from God to a city in Galilee called Nazareth, [27] to a virgin[a]betrothed to a man whose name was Joseph, a descendant of the house of David; and the virgin's name was Mary. [28] And coming to her, the angel said, "Greetings, favored one! The Lord is with you." [29] But she was greatly perplexed at what he said, and kept carefully considering what kind of greeting this was. [30] The angel said to her, "Do not be afraid, Mary, for you have found favor with God. [31] Listen carefully: you will conceive in your womb and give birth to a son, and you shall name Him Jesus. [32] He will be great and eminent and will be called the Son of the Most High; and the Lord God will give Him the throne of His father David; [33] and He will reign over the house of Jacob (Israel) forever, and of His kingdom there shall be no end."

[39] Now at this time Mary arose and hurried to the hill country, to a city of Judah (Judea), [40] and she entered the house of Zacharias and greeted Elizabeth. [41] When Elizabeth heard Mary's greeting, her baby leaped in her womb; and Elizabeth was filled with the Holy Spirit and empowered by Him. [42] And she exclaimed loudly, "Blessed [worthy to be praised] are you among women, and blessed is the fruit of your womb! [43] And how has it happened to me, that the mother of my Lord would come to me? [44] For behold, when the sound of your greeting reached my ears, the baby in my womb leaped for joy. [45] And blessed [spiritually fortunate and favored by God] is she who believed and confidently trusted that there would be a fulfillment of the things that were spoken to her [by the angel sent] from the Lord."

Luke 1:39-45 Amplified Bible (AMP)


Part of being bold is being fearless and not being afraid to be who you are and standing up for what you believe in. When you spend time in God's word, you will grow in confidence and boldness about who you are. You won't need to have an audience to make a statement. Your Priceless attitude will make that statement for you!!

# Things to ponder:

Think of areas you need to be more courageous in and ask God to help you!

_____
_____
_____
_____
_____
_____

When you are challenged in public, how do you respond? What do you feel like people are attacking?

_____
_____
_____
_____
_____
_____

What does boldness mean to you?

09
**CHAPTER NINE**

# You Are Forgiven

Then Peter came up to Him and said, Lord, how many times may my brother sin against me and I forgive him and let it go? [as many as] up to seven times?

Jesus answered him, I tell you, not up to seven times, but seventy times seven!

Matthew 18:21-22 (amp)

If we confess our sins, He is faithful and righteous to forgive us our sins and to cleanse us from all unrighteousness.

1 John 1:9

For I will be merciful and gracious toward their sins and I will remember their deeds of unrighteousness no more.

Hebrews 8:12

Wash me thoroughly [and repeatedly] from my iniquity and guilt and cleanse me and make me wholly pure from my sin!

Psalm 51:2 (AMP)

If we [freely] admit that we have sinned and confess our sins. He is faithful and just (true to His own nature and promises) and will forgive our sins [dismiss our lawlessness] and [continuously] cleanse us from all unrighteousness [everything not in conformity to His will in purpose, thought, and action].

1 John 1:9 (AMP)

**Unconditional.**

There is nothing you can do to separate His love from you.

Ever made a mistake and felt like you were not forgiven? Or like you just weren't the same anymore? The enemy wants nothing more than to make you feel like for every mistake you have made, there is no way out. Well, we know this is not true. God has always forgiven us and always will. He sees us through the blood of Jesus, not for our wrongs, but for our rights standing in Him.

2 AND YOU [HE MADE ALIVE WHEN YOU] WERE [SPIRITUALLY] DEAD AND SEPARATED FROM HIM BECAUSE OF YOUR TRANSGRESSIONS AND SINS, 2 IN WHICH YOU ONCE WALKED. YOU WERE FOLLOWING THE WAYS OF THIS WORLD [INFLUENCED BY THIS PRESENT AGE], IN ACCORDANCE WITH THE PRINCE OF THE POWER OF THE AIR (SATAN), THE SPIRIT WHO IS NOW AT WORK IN THE DISOBEDIENT [THE UNBELIEVING, WHO FIGHT AGAINST THE PURPOSES OF GOD]. 3 AMONG THESE [UNBELIEVERS] WE ALL ONCE LIVED IN THE PASSIONS OF OUR FLESH [OUR BEHAVIOR GOVERNED BY THE SINFUL SELF], INDULGING THE DESIRES OF [A]HUMAN NATURE [WITHOUT THE HOLY SPIRIT] AND [THE IMPULSES] OF THE [SINFUL] MIND. WE WERE, BY NATURE, CHILDREN [UNDER THE SENTENCE] OF [GOD'S] WRATH, JUST LIKE THE REST [OF MANKIND]. 4 BUT GOD, BEING [SO VERY] RICH IN MERCY, BECAUSE OF HIS GREAT AND WONDERFUL LOVE WITH WHICH HE LOVED US, 5 EVEN WHEN WE WERE [SPIRITUALLY] DEAD AND SEPARATED FROM HIM BECAUSE OF OUR SINS, HE MADE US [SPIRITUALLY] ALIVE TOGETHER WITH CHRIST (FOR BY HIS GRACE—HIS UNDESERVED FAVOR AND MERCY—YOU HAVE BEEN SAVED FROM GOD'S JUDGMENT).

EPHESIANS 2:1-5

God shows us this; God forgave us when we were dead in our sins, BUT because of His rich love and mercy towards us, He SAVED us through Christ. There is nothing you can do or will do that you cannot be forgiven for. In the life of Cain and Abel, Cain was filled with jealousy. He killed his brother and tried to hide his sin, but God already knew what happened. Although God drove Cain out, He still marked him so that anyone who attempted to kill him would have sevenfold vengeance returned on his or her life. Who would set a murderer free? Who would protect him? A father, that is who!!! God punished Cain as a consequence for his actions, but he still protected him which is an act of forgiveness. See we may sin, lie, cheat, steal, and have to deal with the repercussions of the actions BUT God will always forgive, love, and protect us.

# Things to ponder:

**Think of a time when someone did something to you that was hurtful or that disappointed you.**

How did you respond?

_____
_____
_____
_____
_____
_____

What could you have done differently? Why?

_____
_____
_____
_____
_____
_____

Did you understand or forgive them? Why or why not?

_____
_____
_____
_____
_____
_____
_____
_____
_____
_____

How can the lens of love affect your future behavior?

_____
_____
_____
_____
_____
_____
_____

What are some areas of your life that you feel that God has not forgiven you for? Why do you feel that He has not forgiven you? Look back over the scripture above and apply them to these areas. You can write them here and see how God has forgiven you.

_____

_____

_____

_____

_____

_____

_____

_____

_____

_____

_____

_____

_____

_____

_____

_____

_____

_____

I remember when I had my daughter out of wedlock. I was so ashamed to return home to Georgia from New York and, of all places, to go to church. See, during my childhood, there were so many family members who just assumed my siblings and I would be statistical failures because we had no mom, and an alcoholic father who worked all the time to support us. Yeah, according to the statistics, we were all on a track to fail out of school, have several kids, be in jail or strung out. So, when I was 28 and pregnant, I felt ashamed at times. I felt like I disappointed God and that I would not be forgiven or loved. It was crazy though because by having her, I began to see how much God did love me. Yet my mind kept telling me, "Hmmm look at you, pregnant, no husband, bringing this baby into the world in an unholy way."

I had to proclaim, "UMMMM STOP! Those negative thoughts have no weight because God said he forgives us even when we do things that are not right or in the best interest for us. He loves me and my baby." Like many others, I had to get into my Word and read how much He loved me and my daughter. She is a blessing, regardless of how she came into the world. Yes, the act of premarital sex is a sin and having her being UNmarried could bring a lot of struggles, but I often thank God for her because seeing her on the sonogram actually made me change my path back to Christ. God forgave me of my sin, and blessed me with my daughter. So, see, my sister, there is nothing you have done sexually, criminally, physically, or mentally that God will not and has not forgiven you for. He knew you would do these things when your eyes veered off of Him or maybe you never knew Him, either way, He knows.

Having my daughter and not being married was no cake walk. I knew her father was not someone I wanted to marry nor was he even good for me, but when you're in sin, it does feel good. You may not want to admit it, but it was fun. I struggled with her for a while until God sent someone into my life while she was a baby that helped me along the way (he is now my husband). I was single and alone with a daughter. I didn't have a mother to guide me along the way and since I loss her so young, I was somewhat lost and clueless. Thank God that my family supported us along the way, especially, my sister who helped me raise her for almost two years—well, heck, she did raise her. I was filled with so much fear and panic that on some days, I couldn't function. My sister, who had two boys, swept right in and took care of her when I couldn't. The guilt I felt for not being married, not providing her with a proper home structure, and not giving her a functioning family unit made me sad. No kid deserves longing for her father and not understanding why he won't come around.

But thank God for His love because in Him, I saw that He had my back. I changed my direction and put my life back on the path with Christ and His word. It was just that easy; change your thoughts and know that He loves you. Turn back to what's in you and He will be right there. It is like He was saying, "I have been waiting. Let's pick up where we left off." So, forgive yourself, change your mind, and keep it moving! There is nothing that can stop God's plan and love for you!

**10**
**CHAPTER TEN**

# Who Am I?

So God created man in His own image in the image and likeness of God He created him male and female He created them, I am not my own, I am a woman of purity.

Genesis 1:27

_____
_____
_____
_____
_____
_____
_____
_____
_____
_____
_____
_____
_____
_____
_____
_____

**You Are**
**Custom Made**

You are more than enough. You are His handiwork. You are a Priceless Jewel.

You may answer this by saying: a cheerleader, a dancer, an athlete, a mother, a wife, a scholar? No these are all attributes of who you are because of Jesus.

The following Love Notes show us who we really are:

| | |
|---:|---|
| Genesis 1:27 | So God created man in His own image, in the image and likeness of God He created him, male and fe-male He created them. |
| Romans 8:17 | And if we are [His] children, then we are [His] heirs also, heirs of God and fellow heirs with Christ [sharing His inheritance with Him} only we must share His suffering if we are to share His glory. |
| Romans 8:37 | Yet amid all these things we are more than conquerors and gain a surpassing victory through Him who loved us. |
| 2 Corinthians 5:20 | We are therefore Christ's ambassadors, as though God were making his appeal through us. We implore you on Christ's behalf: Be reconciled to God. |
| 1 Peter 2:9 | But you are a chosen race, a royal priesthood a dedicated nation [God's] own purchased, special people that you may set forth the wonderful deeds and display the virtues and perfections of Him who called you out of darkness into His marvelous light. |
| 2 Corinthians 5:21 | For our sake, He made Christ [ virtually] to be sin Who knew no sin, so that in and through Him we might become endued with, viewed as being in, examples of the righteousness of God [what we ought to be, approved and acceptable and in right relationship with Him, by His goodness]. |
| James 4:7 | So be subject to God, Resist the devil [stand firm against him] and he will fall from you. |
| Colossians 1:21-22 | And although you were at one time estranged and alienated from Him and were of hostile attitude of mind in your wicked activities yet now has [Christ the Messiah] reconciled [ you to God] in the body of His flesh through death, in order to present you holy and faithfulness and irreproachable in His [the Father's presence. |

| | |
|---|---|
| EPHESIANS 2:10 | For we are God's [own] handiwork (His workmanship) recreated in Christ Jesus (born anew) that we may do those good works which God predestined (planned beforehand) for us [taking paths which He prepared ahead of time] that we should walk in them [living the good life which He prearranged and make ready for us to live]. |

When you see yourself how God sees you, you begin to realize it's not your title or social club that makes you unique, but it's your relationship with God, the purity of your heart, the kindness you show others, and the compassion you share when others make mistakes. It is God who makes you who you are.

Being a young woman of God is a daily walk, not a Sunday outfit. It is a lifestyle. Your life will display the attributes of Christ.

| | |
|---|---|
| GENESIS 1:27 1 | So God created man in His own image in the image and likeness of God He created him male and female He created them, I am not my own, I am a woman of purity. |
| 1 CORINTHIANS 6:19 | Do you not know that your body is a temple of the Holy Spirit who is within you, whom you have [received as a gift] from God, and that you are not your own [property]? |
| ROMANS 12:2 | Do not be conformed to this world (this age) [fashioned after and adapted to its external, superficial customs] but be transformed (changed) by the [entire] renewal of your mind [by its new ideals and its new attitude] so that you may prove [for yourselves] what is the good and acceptable and perfect will of God even the thing which is good and acceptable and perfect [in His sight for you]. |
| COLOSSIANS 3:2 | And set your minds and keep them set on what is above (the higher things), not on the things that are on the earth. |

Your body is not your own. The Word of God teaches us to flee from sexual immorality and sensual idolatry. When we honor our bodies, we understand that God owns us and that our bodies belong to him until the day of marriage. As Priceless Jewels, we must honor our bodies. When someone respects you, they hold value in what you value. When you respect and value yourself, then others will do so, and if they don't, you still must be who you are. Why compromise your purity for anyone? This is something you can never get back. True love will wait. If this man or guy loves you, he will honor your desires and not be so sex driven. This is why healthy boundaries are necessary if dating. Set the expectation from the beginning and don't entertain anything different. A person can't miss nor crave what they never had.

For every young woman who has given up her virginity like I did, know this, God forgives you and can heal you from all that hurt. For my sister who is allowing that man to be with you without marrying you, stop! You can decide right now to recommit your body to God and wait until you're married. Show that man how much you value yourself and remember, real true love waits. Ask yourself these questions: Does this man, or boy, remind you of the gentleman of Jesus? Does he honor you? Does he care for you regardless of what he gets? What you're giving him, he cannot purchase at any store or be duplicated. Your body is valuable and you must hold yourself to the value that God assigned to you when He created you. Any man can find a rock on the street and pick it up, but for a Priceless Jewel, he would have to dig real deep in the depths of the earth where not many people go in order to find something so rare. Then a certain amount of work would have to go into it before the gem is revealed. If he values you, he will take the time to dig and build a foundation with you and then marry you. He will wait. Value who you are, for if you don't, who will? After all, God will see you no differently. Remember, he sees you through the eyes of Christ- washed in His blood and cleansed from all sin, why not honor the one who honors you? Seeing God's love for you should draw you in and make you not want to sin again; it should make you want to have an attitude of thanksgiving, like a kid who was rewarded for constantly doing good. Remember, this sex is NOT love!! Each time you have sex with a man that is not your husband, you open yourself up to everyone he was with and everyone his partner was with, so on and so forth. So, sleeping with one person who slept with two people who slept with two people means you have slept with five people already. Actually, more than that because you didn't calculate the people they slept with. Imagine if he slept with 20 people who slept with 50 people. You can stop this cycle and start brand new. Take time to purify your heart and renew your mind back to the things of God. Wait for your king.

I share this not to judge or to condemn, but because I love you. I often wonder why do we, as women, not value our virginity more. Let me speak for myself: Why did I, as a young woman, a high school junior, have sex for the first time? Why did I allow a stranger, who I was only dating for 8 months, receive my virginity?

I will tell you why; it is because I didn't understand what true love was or who I was. I thought that this man would marry me and honor me and love me. Ummm Kristine why would I think that? If he loved and honored me he would not have asked to have sex in the first place. Secondly, I started to pay too much attention to sex, foreplay, and everything that came with it. All I wanted to do was be loved and looked at as if I was special. Maybe that is not your situation. See I won't blame my lack of a mother or my father's addiction for the reasons why I had sex. I own my part in it because I chose to put myself in situations when I knew better.

I became empty once my high school "boyfriend" left me after a year. I was so hurt and lost that I could not get back what was so precious and unique to me. All of this for a 20 second feel and the thought "that I was loved". Trying to be grown too fast, desiring what I saw on TV, or in my friends' lives led to giving someone something that did not belong to me. What you give your attention to, you will become or do. I have had some people tell me there is nothing wrong with having sex before marriage or dating this guy and that guy. After all, you have to know what you like. Ummm, all you're doing is comparing the sex of this one with that one and it's all empty and void of love.

The only person who truly loves you is Jesus! He can love you like no other. Your body is not a candy shop where people come get samples and leave. Over time, that store will be empty. Your hearth will become hard and alone. You will begin to wonder: Why won't he stay? Am I enough? Am I pretty? What do I have to do to keep him? We must have a standard that we live by. Look at Esther in the bible, she was chosen to be Queen over all of the other beautiful and talented women that came before the king and she didn't have to sleep with him to gain status. Ladies and young girls, you are so precious, you're more than eye candy or an arm trophy; you are a Priceless Jewel, the daughter of the KING!

# Things to ponder:

**Think about the following and define.**

What is purity?

_____
_____
_____
_____
_____
_____

What is love?

_____
_____
_____
_____
_____
_____
_____

**Look through the bible and see what God says about these two words: love and purity. Purity is not just in the area of sex, but also in integrity. It is also about helping people stay pure.**

Has something you said or done become a stumbling block in someone else's life? If so, pray and ask God to restore that area and help you to have a pure heart.

List some areas that you feel you need to work on and find a Love Note that you can stand on.

1.

2.

3.

4.

5.

6.

How can you set boundaries in your life in order to walk a life of purity?

_____
_____
_____
_____
_____
_____

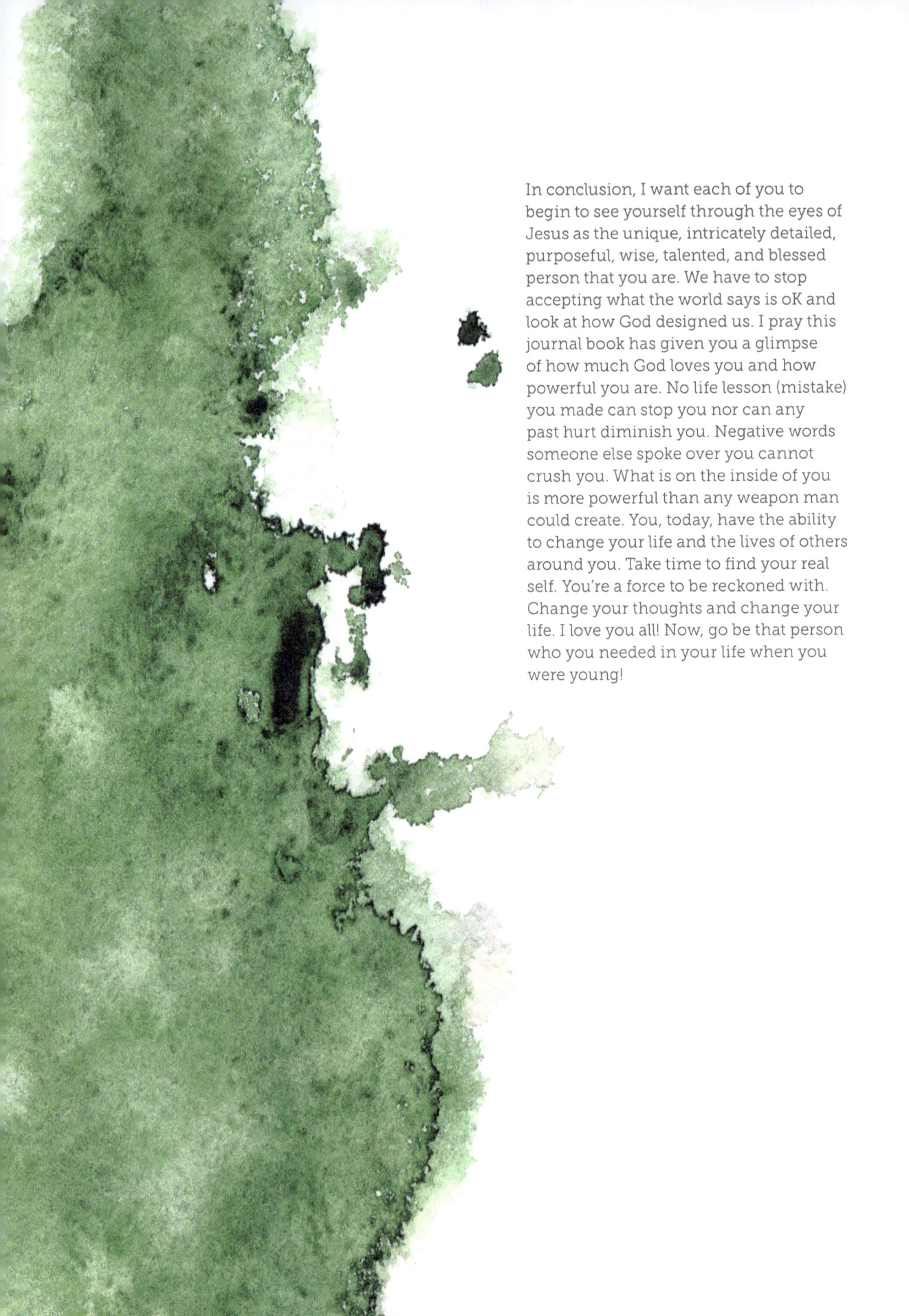

In conclusion, I want each of you to begin to see yourself through the eyes of Jesus as the unique, intricately detailed, purposeful, wise, talented, and blessed person that you are. We have to stop accepting what the world says is oK and look at how God designed us. I pray this journal book has given you a glimpse of how much God loves you and how powerful you are. No life lesson (mistake) you made can stop you nor can any past hurt diminish you. Negative words someone else spoke over you cannot crush you. What is on the inside of you is more powerful than any weapon man could create. You, today, have the ability to change your life and the lives of others around you. Take time to find your real self. You're a force to be reckoned with. Change your thoughts and change your life. I love you all! Now, go be that person who you needed in your life when you were young!

# Prayer of Salvation

We confess out of our mouths that Jesus Christ is Lord and that He came to earth as a man to fulfil the law and conquer sin. He died in our place so that we won't have to pay the ultimate price we so deserved.

[9] BECAUSE IF YOU ACKNOWLEDGE AND CONFESS WITH YOUR MOUTH THAT JESUS IS LORD [RECOGNIZING HIS POWER, AUTHORITY, AND MAJESTY AS GOD], AND BELIEVE IN YOUR HEART THAT GOD RAISED HIM FROM THE DEAD, YOU WILL BE SAVED. [10] FOR WITH THE HEART A PERSON BELIEVES [IN CHRIST AS SAVIOR] RESULTING IN HIS JUSTIFICATION [THAT IS, BEING MADE RIGHTEOUS—BEING FREED OF THE GUILT OF SIN AND MADE ACCEPTABLE TO GOD]; AND WITH THE MOUTH HE ACKNOWLEDGES AND CONFESSES [HIS FAITH OPENLY], RESULTING IN AND CONFIRMING [HIS] SALVATION.

ROMANS 10:9-10 AMPLIFIED BIBLE (AMP)

**Father in the name of Jesus, I confess that I was a sinner and that you died on the cross for me and rose on the third day. Lord, I ask you to come into my heart and life as my Lord and Personal savior, heal me, cleanse me, and make me whole.**

**In Jesus' name,**
**Amen!!**

---

If you prayed this prayer, you have just changed your life! Heaven is celebrating the salvation of your soul. From this day forward, you are a new creation in Christ, no matter what mistake you made, whether it was 15 minutes ago or fifteen years ago, it is washed white as snow. I highly recommend that you connect with a church that teaches the gospel of grace so that you can grow further in your walk with Christ.

Please visit: www.kristinejones.org for booking, sowing donations, or to show support.

Office number 404-226-3176
Email info@kristinejones.org

With love Kristine Jones

www.ingramcontent.com/pod-product-compliance
Lightning Source LLC
Chambersburg PA
CBHW061821290426
44110CB00027B/2936